STOCKTON-ON-TEES
A Pictorial History

St Peter's church

STOCKTON ~ ON ~ TEES
A Pictorial History

Robert Woodhouse

Phillimore

1989

Published by
PHILLIMORE & CO. LTD.
Shopwyke Hall, Chichester, Sussex

ISBN 0 85033 720 8

Printed and bound in Great Britain by
BIDDLES LTD.
Guildford, Surrey

List of Illustrations

Illustration Acknowledgements

Robert Woodhouse would like to acknowledge the use of photographs in this book as follows: Cleveland County Council, Libraries and Leisure Department, for nos. 1-10, 12-57, 66-94, 96-124, 126-181; Cleveland County Council, Economic Development and Planning Department, for no. 11; Mrs. R. Hill, whose father was Estate Manager and Bailiff for the Raimes family who lived at Hartburn Lodge, for nos. 134-144; Mrs. F. Britton for nos. 74-77; Mrs. M. Dalkin for nos. 145, 146; Mr. and Mrs. K. Thomas for nos. 58-65, 95; Mrs. D. Prince for no. 125.

Acknowledgements

Most enterprises are a team effort and I am indebted to a number of people for their assistance with the many aspects of this book.

Mrs. Joyce Chesney and Miss Anita Brown provide excellent service to the public at Stockton Reference Library and I am most grateful to them for finding the time, energy and patience to supply me with a great deal of advice and information.

Many of the photographs are from Stockton Library's collection and others were loaned by people from their private collections. Dave Morrell copied and, in a number of cases, improved the quality of these original prints, and also provided the colour photograph for the front cover and portrait photograph. I am indebted to him for producing photographs of such high quality, along with a range of practical advice and realistic comment.

Mrs. Valerie Symonds has typed correspondence relating to the book as well as the text itself. She continues to provide a swift typing service of the highest quality for which I am most grateful.

Several people have co-operated by supplying photographs for use in the book and their co-operation and generosity is greatly appreciated. Staff of the Cleveland County Library Service allowed use of photographs in their local collection, Mrs. R. Hill of Saltburn provided the photographs of Hartburn Lodge; Mrs. Dalkin of Linthorpe, Hartburn School groups; Ken and Doreen Thomas of Middlesbrough, the John Walker photographs; Mrs. F. Britton of Stockton, Castle Theatre materials; Mrs. D. Prince of Brompton near Northallerton, the children's ward of Stockton and Thornaby Hospital. Many of these photographs are previously unpublished and it is particularly gratifying that these people are keen for such material to be published before it is perhaps lost for ever when family archives disappear or are destroyed.

Staff from Cleveland County's Archaeological Service have provided advice and information and with their assistance every effort had been made to ensure the accuracy of the text.

Introduction

Cleveland's early settlers kept to high ground away from the meandering course of the River Tees. Dr. Frank Elgee identified many moorland sites in his publication *Early Man in North East Yorkshire* (1930) and in recent years Cleveland's County Archaeology Department has carried out further detailed investigations into Bronze and Iron Age settlements, often in conjunction with aerial surveys (for example, *Cleveland History from the Air* by M. M. Brown and L. Still, and *Recent Excavations in Cleveland* by Cleveland County Archaeology Section).

Using York as a main base, the Romans finally subdued this area in A.D. 71 and garrison towns were established at places such as Malton and Piercebridge as part of a communications network linked with Hadrian's Wall in the north. Central Cleveland seems to have been largely untouched by the Roman occupation but there is extensive evidence of Iron Age and Romano-British settlements close to the Tees at places such as Ingleby, Barwick and Thorpe Thewles. The chance discovery of an Anglo-Saxon cemetery at Norton in 1982 was followed by excavations during 1984 and 1985 which uncovered the largest pagan burial ground in the north of England. This site lies about two miles from the centre of Stockton and the discovery of glass beads, spears and shields, along with 120 skeletons, indicates that there was a flourishing settlement in this locality between A.D. 450 and 650.

During the tenth century, the Anglo-Saxon estate centred around Norton was given to the Bishop of Durham by a son of the Earl of Northumberland as a mark of his high regard for St Cuthbert, patron saint of the bishopric. St Mary's church at Norton is the only surviving cruciform Saxon church in the north of England and much of the original crossing tower and north transept survives intact. The parish of Norton covered approximately fifteen square miles along the north bank of the Tees and Stockton was one of a number of small settlements within its boundaries. It remained part of the parish of Norton until the early 18th century.

The first documentary reference to Stockton appears in the Boldon Book of 1183, the Palatinate of Durham's equivalent of Domesday Book. The name Stockton indicates a 'tun' or 'village' belonging to the 'stoc' or 'monastery' (of the Bishop of Durham). This survey recorded that there were 11 villeins and six and a half farmers on the land at Stockton, and it also reveals that Stockton had a hall which was used by the Bishop during his tour of the diocese.

The manor of Stockton was created shortly after 1183 and in 1189 it was purchased by Bishop Pudsey, along with the royal manor of Sadberge. No documentary evidence is available to indicate when Stockton gained a Charter of Incorporation, but it is thought that the Bishop of Durham made the town 'a borough by prescription' in the middle of the 13th century. At that time Stockton, planned and planted by the Bishop to compete with Yarm and Hartlepool, was increasing in importance as a port and business centre and there was also considerable growth in population, for Bishop Thomas Hatfield's survey of 1384 mentions *tenentes infra burgum* and *tenentes extra burgum* – meaning those living within the borough and those outside. This survey also records that 'Richard Maurice and his associates hold the farm of the borough' – it seems likely that these people were the mayor and aldermen of that time. The term mayor is not mentioned until 1495 when Robert Burdon held the office and his name appears on panels in the entrance to the parish church.

The Bishop's manor house covered a large site at the southern end of the High Street overlooking the river. King John is said to have stayed there during 1214 in the company of Bishop Poicteu, and alterations were carried out on the orders of Bishop Richard Kellow in 1310. Scottish raiders caused considerable damage in this area during the 14th century and following further building work in 1376 the Bishop's residence became known as Stockton Castle. There was another period of renovation under Bishop Langley (1406-37) and he paid some eighty visits to the town during this period.

In 1574 an inquiry reported that the building was 'decaied and ruynous', with a total of £1,600 needed to repair the castle. Four years later Bishop Barnes ordered more repairs and building work to be carried out. During 1597 Bishop Matthew spent time convalescing at Stockton, but in the same year the castle was damaged by fire. Royalists garrisoned the castle during the early stages of the English Civil War, but in 1644 Scottish forces moved in and when Parliament met in October 1645 it was decided to dispose of castle lands and materials. On 24 March 1648 the Manor of Stockton was sold to William Underwood and James Nelthorpe for £6,165 10s. 2½d., but it was another four years before Parliament ordered its demolition. The only building to remain on the site was a castellated barn which stood in Castle Field near Bridge Road. On 29 June 1865 it was demolished, but an archaeological excavation in the summer of 1966 unearthed evidence of occupation on the castle site between the 12th and the 16th centuries. According to the parish register for 1666 there were 'but 120 dwelling houses' in Stockton and 'none of them brick'. Much of the stonework from Stockton Castle was re-used during building schemes that took place during the Hanoverian period and, before redevelopment of the High Street's east side in the early 1970s, it was possible to identify some of this 'dressed' stonework in lower levels of buildings on Castlegate, Silver Street and Finkle Street.

By the mid-18th century, Stockton had taken on the appearance of a thriving Hanoverian township. During 1699 a Presbyterian Meeting House and a Shambles had been opened and in 1713 the new parish of Stockton was founded. The parish church was opened and consecrated on a site at the north end of the High Street, close to the chapel of ease which had previously served as a place of worship. Sir Christopher Wren's work probably influenced the architect of this fine brick-built church which has seen many alterations to the interior over the years. Galleries were added in 1719, 1748 and 1827, but they made the interior much darker. Extensive restoration work was carried out during the early 1890s. This included the reglazing of 14 windows and the removal of old box pews, along with a section of the galleries. The overall effect was to lighten the church considerably, and a further change was to move the pulpit from a central position to the north side. It was either at this time or in 1906 that the fine triple-decker pulpit was reduced to a double-decker. A chancel was added as part of this Edwardian scheme and in 1925 a side or lady chapel was built on to the south nave aisle. Another extensive restoration scheme was completed during the early 1980s and this fine building was re-dedicated by the Archbishop of York on 11 June 1984.

The first mention of the Mayor's House at Stockton is made in Hatfield's survey of 1384 and it was probably rebuilt in the late 15th century. By the late 17th century the traditional Mayor's House had given way to part accommodation in a stone-built tollbooth on the High Street. Careful investigations during 1985 revealed that the tollbooth measured thirteen yards by seven yards with a flight of steps attached to the western end of the building. Public announcements and proclamations were made from these steps and between here and the Shambles (of 1699) stood a single-storey covered cross which was built in 1709.

During 1735 a new Town House was built on the site of the tollbooth and nine years later further reconstruction work added an inn, cellars and four bow-fronted shops. Over the last 250 years there has been talk of demolition and replacement, but this impressive building has survived to accommodate a series of famous events. On 18 September 1810, 72 gentlemen celebrated the opening of a cut in the River Tees between Portrack and Stockton and in May 1822 there was more banqueting to celebrate the laying of the first rail of what was to become the Stockton and Darlington Railway. The arrival of *Locomotion No. 1* at Stockton on 27 September 1825 was cause for yet more merry-making in the Town House, but the most spectacular occasion of all must have been the reception for the Duke of Wellington on 24 September 1827 when floral displays and lamps provided background decoration. The council chamber was reconstructed during 1880 and further restoration and refurbishment work was carried out on the whole building during 1985 to coincide with the 250th anniversary of its original foundation.

Since the 1960s, the central section of Stockton's wide High Street has been the setting for a twice-weekly market, but other venues were used previously and market charters were granted to the town in 1310, 1602 and 1666. Just south of the Town House stands a doric column which was erected by John Short in 1768 at a cost of £45. It replaced an earlier covered cross and on its steps the hirings took place each year on the Wednesdays before 13 May and 23 November. At this event farm labourers bound themselves to their employers for the following six months. A few yards south of the market cross stands the Shambles which is dated 1825 and represents the third such building to stand on this site. Buildings on the west side of the High Street are surprisingly uniform in width, reflecting the planned origin of the town. A report in 1500 stated that 'according to ancient custom' these frontages measured 20 ft. – indeed they remain so today.

Stockton's growing importance as a commercial and business centre during the 18th century produced a number of locally-born characters from different walks of life who gained national recognition. Joseph Reed was born in Stockton in March 1723 and he supplemented his main income from a rope-making business by writing poetry and plays. During 1757 Reed moved his business to London where his writings enjoyed mixed success. A tragedy entitled *Madrigal and Trulletta* was performed at Covent Garden Theatre in 1758, but it was badly received by critics. A farce, *The Register Office*, had a good run at the Drury Lane Theatre in 1761 and *Tom Jones*, a comic opera adapted from Fielding's work, also enjoyed a fair measure of success.

Joseph Ritson was born and brought up in Stockton during the mid-18th century, but in 1775 he joined a conveyancing firm in London. Five years later he began his own business as a conveyancer in Gray's Inn and in 1789 he was called to the bar. Away from business matters, Ritson had a consuming interest in ancient literature, poetry and drama. He became one of the earliest collectors of local verse and published a number of northern collections during the 1780s and early 1790s.

Brass Crosby was born in Stockton on 8 May 1725 and after training in the North East he moved to London where he served for a number of years as an attorney. During the

1760s he held offices such as councillor, sheriff and alderman before his election as Lord Mayor of London on 29 September 1770. Crosby soon became involved in a struggle with the House of Commons over press coverage of parliamentary proceedings and this resulted in his imprisonment in the Tower of London, but he was released, amid great popular rejoicing, on 8 May 1771. A ruling given in his favour stated that in future there was to be no attempt to restrain the publication of parliamentary debates.

There was a strong Baptist community in Stockton during the 18th century and prominent among this group was Thomas Sheraton. Born in 1751, he gained employment as a journeyman cabinet-maker in one of the larger timber firms or raftyards in the area. His strong religious convictions led to publication in 1782 of a tract entitled *A Scriptural Illustration of the Doctrine of Regeneration*. Other religious leaders paid little attention to his writings, but Sheraton's skill as an artist and draughtsman was soon appreciated. His engraving of the south end of Stockton High Street was published in 1787 and more time was spent teaching and designing over the next few years. There were not enough outlets for his publications on design work in his native North East and Sheraton moved his family to London in about 1790. Shortly after arriving in the capital, he published a collection of 84 large folio plates entitled *Design for Furniture*, and during the early 1790s *The Cabinet Maker and Upholsterers' Drawing Book* appeared. Sheraton spent the first few years of the 19th century in Stockton where he was minister of the Baptist congregation and in 1803 he published *The Cabinet Dictionary*. Plans for an encyclopaedia of cabinet-making did not work out and he slipped into poverty. The strain of years of overwork began to tell, his health deteriorated and Thomas Sheraton died in October 1806. It was some forty years later that the significance of his work was truly appreciated.

Few 18th-century buildings survive in central Stockton, but several buildings on Finkle Street were constructed and faced with stone from Stockton Castle after its demolition in 1652. Other nearby properties were constructed with limestone from the Durham area or sandstone from further up the Tees. A narrow entrance leads into Green Dragon Yard and within this yard stood the borough pound or pinfold where stray animals were impounded and cockfighting took place in a cockpit.

At the north end of Green Dragon Yard stands a building that was originally the tithe barn of the Bishops of Durham, but in 1765 it was converted into a playhouse. Thomas Bates and his group of travelling players gave the first performance at the theatre in 1766 and the enterprise prospered for 20 years under Bates' management. His nephew, James Cawdell, ran the theatre from 1786 until his retirement in 1798 and it was then rented to Stephen Kemble, a member of the famous theatrical family. He did much to improve the theatre building and his appearances as Falstaff were particularly notable for he weighed some thirty stone. Kemble's departure in July 1815 was followed by frequent changes of management during the next two decades, but a highlight during 1833 was the appearance of Paganini. Prices more than doubled for this one night's musical entertainment, but when the performance began the building was filled to capacity. By 1858 the theatre had been renamed the Royal, but the quality of entertainment had fallen, along with admission prices, and when the New Theatre Royal opened in Yarm Lane on 6 August 1866 its days were numbered. By 1870 it had become 'a penny gaff of the worst description' and during the summer of 1874 local Salvation Army members opened it as a People's Hall. The building was then occupied by a confectionery company but after an extensive programme of restoration work the premises were re-opened as a theatre and exhibition centre on 29 April 1980.

John Walker was born on 29 May 1781 at 104 High Street, and an early education in the town gave him considerable knowledge of chemistry, botany and mineralogy. Further studies at Durham and London saw him qualify as a surgeon, but after returning to Stockton this jovial little man set up in business as a druggist at 59 High Street. Although phosphorous had been discovered in 1669, a means of igniting a suitable compound by single friction eluded him and others until 1826. During that year John Walker produced a flame on three-inch splints which had been dipped in a chemical mixture and the first recorded sale appears in his day book on 7 April 1827.

By 23 September 1829 sales of 23,206 friction lights had been recorded in his day book. They were sold for one shilling per hundred (plus two pence for a case), along with a small piece of glass paper which was used to create the surfaces needed for ignition by friction. John Walker moved to a house overlooking the Green behind the parish church and in February 1858 he retired from business. He died there in May 1859 without bothering to patent his invention, leaving others to make their fortunes from his research work.

The West Durham coalfield expanded rapidly during the late 18th century and in 1767 a scheme was put forward to distribute its output by way of the Tees Valley towns. In the years that followed, Robert Whitworth and James Brindley surveyed a canal route, but by 1810 the canal had still not been constructed and support increased for an alternative railway project. A group of landowners, business men and bankers gave their backing to the scheme and George Overton surveyed a line for the railway in 1818. Three years later George Stephenson was commissioned to re-survey the route and his recommendations were adopted. These included the suggestion that steam locomotives could support the use of horses on the level stretches of the line.

Construction of the railway from Witton Park Colliery to the quayside at Stockton took nearly four years and cost almost double Stephenson's original estimate of about £60,000. On 13 May 1822, Thomas Meynell of Yarm, Chairman of the Stockton and Darlington Railway Company, laid the first section of track at St John's Well Crossing alongside Bridge Road in Stockton. For centuries, this well had supplied part of the town with drinking water, but the site is dominated by a brick building which has been described as the ticket office for the railway. Stephenson and his hordes of navvies learned valuable lessons during the construction of the line, which features in transport history as the first public railway in the world to employ steam locomotives. The line was officially opened on 27 September 1825, and in 1830 a suspension bridge was constructed across the Tees to extend the line to Middlesbrough.

Industrial expansion during the 18th and 19th centuries brought other improvements in communication. A ferry service linked Stockton with the township of South Stockton (now known as Thornaby), but in August 1764 the foundations of 'the old Stone Bridge' were laid. It had five arches and was opened in April 1769 at an original cost of £8,000. This outlay was defrayed by a system of tolls on traffic and pedestrians, but although the cost of the structure had been met by 1816, the tolls were not abolished until 1820.

River transport, base of the town's prosperity from its medieval foundation, played an increasingly important part as the centuries passed and by September 1810 the cut in the Mandale loop of the river had been completed at a cost of £12,163 5s. 4d. In 1828 authorisation was given for a further cut in the river at Portrack. By this time Stockton had gained importance as a shipbuilding centre and, as well as completing a large number of colliers, Stockton shipyards built vessels for the Royal and Merchant Navies. In 1776/7 the Mark Pye Yard launched the frigates *Bellona* and *Preston* for Government service, and during the 1790s Haw's Yard built some forty vessels, the largest of which, *Highland Lass*, weighed 566 tons. A number of associated trades benefited from the increase in shipbuilding and firms at Yarm and Stockton supplied materials such as linen cloth and sailcloth for vessels built in North-East ports. During 1767 some 64,000 yards of sailcloth were exported from the port of Stockton. Ropery Street, which runs off the west side of the High Street, is a reminder of the days when ropemaking was a flourishing local business. Rope works are shown on early maps in this area of central Stockton and also at nearby Hartburn.

River-based industries continued to flourish in the mid-19th century and in 1854 Richardson, Duck & Company launched the Tees' first iron vessel, a screw steamer *Advance*. Another ship named *Iron Age* soon followed and the 1860s brought a spate of shipbuilding with the emphasis on size. The *Zaire*, the largest vessel of its type to be launched on the river, left the yard of Messrs. Pearce Company at Stockton on 13 November 1860 and within the next few months the *Palikan*, a large screw steamer, was launched from Richardson & Company's yard at South Stockton. The census of 1851 showed a total of 101 men employed in shipbuilding at Stockton, but ten years later the number of shipyard workers had almost doubled. During the 1870s much of the area's manufactured iron was used for ships' angles and plates, but the closing years of the 19th century brought problems to yards in the Stockton area as shipbuilding moved further down river.

In 1820 an Act of Parliament was obtained for 'Lighting, Cleansing and otherwise improving the Town and Borough of Stockton'. This was necessary because the north end of the built-up area was administered by the vicar and his 12 vestrymen while the southern sector was governed separately by the Mayor and his eight aldermen. Two years later gas was installed, with the gasworks occupying the corner of Yarm Lane and Bridge Road, and in the same year the town's first police officer was appointed.

Many towns in the North of England were badly affected by the cholera outbreak of 1831. It began in the port of Sunderland during October and spread south towards Stockton where local inhabitants had to take precautions in an attempt to limit its effects. Windows were whitewashed, doors and woodwork got a coating of tar and a fund was opened to provide food for those in need, but during the summer of 1832 some 604 people out of a total population of 7,800 contracted the disease. Within weeks, 126 victims had died and a communal grave was hastily excavated on the edge of the township. Another outbreak of cholera in 1849 resulted in 20 deaths and another communal grave was dug on the south side of Trinity church. A circle of trees marked the site and several of these are still standing. During 1854 there was a further outbreak of cholera, but on this occasion there were few deaths.

During the 19th century housing was packed into sectors of land close to the High Street and adjacent to the river. Narrow streets with names such as Cherry Lane, Sugarhouse Opening and Housewife's Lane were a feature of the Thistle Green area. Constable's Yard was typical of several such yards that were situated to the east of the High Street, but by the beginning of this century these quaint collections of housing had degenerated into slums.

The High Street area changed considerably during the 19th century. Almshouses had been built on an island site at the south-west end in 1662. They were to cater 'for the convenient lodging of poor impotent persons belonging to the Township of Stockton', but in 1816 the site was cleared and a new building was erected. It had a dispensary and a penny bank where amounts from as little as one halfpenny could be deposited although interest was not credited until the account had reached 16s. 8d. In 1896 this building was demolished and a new almshouse was opened on Dovecot Street. The impressive Victoria

Buildings were erected on the site during the closing years of last century.

A number of coaching inns, such as the *Black Lion* and the *Vane Arms*, were included in the south-eastern section of the High Street. Regular carrier services linked these premises with market centres in North Yorkshire and County Durham. Public pumps were situated at either end of the High Street and water sellers hawked supplies around the street at a cost of ½d. per pail. Water was also obtained from the river at low tide when it was relatively clean and free of salt.

The Borough Hall was built in 1852 on the opposite side of the High Street. It represented one of the best furnished places of entertainment in the North of England and included a dining hall which was also used to stage shows and bazaars, as well as a main hall measuring 80 feet by 60 feet. Further seating on the balcony gave a total capacity for 700 people.

Rogers Engineering Works was established in 1765 on a site behind the south-western sector of the High Street and it is believed that they supplied the world's first steam plough to the Fiskin Brothers in 1855. The machine was exhibited at a nearby farm called 'Bowes Field' and the patent was then sold to John Fowler of Leeds who manufactured an improved version of the plough for more than sixty years.

Many of the town's early chapels were situated in the area of West Row. Baptists opened a small chapel in West Row in 1809 and, after enlarging the building in 1840, they moved to new premises in Wellington Street in 1869. A final move to the present red-brick building took place in 1902. The nearby Unitarian church was erected in 1872 and Brunswick Methodist chapel in Dovecot Street dates from 1823.

Stockton's population increased from 10,172 in 1851 to a total of 51,478 in 1901. Numbered among these was William Thomson Hay, who was born at 23 Durham Street on 6 December 1888. His family soon left the area, but Will Hay became one of the most successful British music hall stars to enter films. He was particularly noted for schoolroom sketches where he played a tyrannical yet hopeless schoolmaster and some of his films, such as 'Oh Mr. Porter' and 'The Black Sheep of Whitehall', became great classics of the British cinema.

The growing township gained a range of improved services during the 1870s and 1880s. A public library service began in 1877 and six years later a fire station was built in West Row. Before this time the horse-drawn firefighting equipment was based in a corner of the parish churchyard and firefighters were summoned by the tolling of a bell in the cupola of the Town House. Stockton Surgical Hospital was established in 1862 in a building close to the quayside. Only five patients could be cared for in these premises so in 1875 the foundation stone of a new building was laid at a site on Bowesfield Lane. The first patients were admitted to the Stockton and Thornaby Hospital some two years later.

For a number of years Stockton remained the lowest bridging point on the Tees, and Victoria Bridge was opened in 1887 to replace the earlier structure of 1769. For several decades passenger steamers travelled between Stockton and Middlesbrough until the towns were linked by trams. Pleasure outings ran from Stockton to Tees Bay, Seaton Snook on the north bank of the estuary and southwards down the coastline as far as Whitby. Many of Stockton's menfolk were employed in foundries or shipyards on the opposite bank of the river and used Kelley's Ferry to make the short river crossing to and from their workplace. It ran from Sugar House Green and Cleveland Row on the Stockton bank across to the end of Trafalgar Street in Thornaby and the fare is said never to have increased to more than ½d. per passenger.

The war years (1914-18) brought the same pattern of changes that affected other northern towns – recruiting drives for the armed services, increased industrial output, and women moving into previously male-dominated occupations. A stream of refugees and injured servicemen arrived at local railway stations and the stark horror of war was highlighted dramatically by the bombardment of nearby Hartlepool in December 1914. Local morale was lifted during the war by the actions of Sgt. Edward Cooper during the third battle of Ypres in th summer of 1917. His courage and bravery led to the capture of an enemy blockhouse which was holding up British troops, and in September 1917 he received the Victoria Cross from King George V at Buckingham Palace. After the war he returned to his home town and played an important part in local matters as a magistrate and as an officer in the Home Guard.

Several prominent buildings in the High Street, Church Road and Bishopton Lane areas date from the early years of this century, but not far away on either side of the High Street living conditions had deteriorated badly. Voluntary workers made sustained efforts to improve amenities for deprived families, but real progress was only made with the appointment of Dr. G. C. M. M'Gonigle as the town's Medical Officer of Health in 1924. He achieved national fame as a writer, speaker and practitioner on the subject of malnutrition and in 1938 he published a standard work entitled *Poverty and Public Health*. Dr. M'Gonigle developed a special knowledge of orthopaedic work and, after taking a particular interest in crippled people, he reduced both the infant mortality rate and the number of crippled children in the township.

A programme of slum clearance was initiated in the 1920s and families were moved to the northern perimeter of Stockton. The Depression years brought further hardship to Stockton and shipyards closed with the loss of many jobs. In 1932 Blair's Engineering Works ended over ninety years' production with the loss of 1,600 jobs, and, in 1935, 250 local people marched to London where they delivered a petition to Parliament in protest against unemployment and the Means Test.

The establishment of I.C.I. Ltd. at Billingham during the inter-war years brought much-needed employment to the whole area and a number of new road schemes improved communications with other local centres. Church Road, known in earlier days as Church Row and Paradise Row, has seen several reconstructions, including an important one in 1937 which provided direct access from the High Street to Portrack Lane.

During the last 50 years, Stockton's boundaries have spread northwards and westwards to link up with places such as Norton and Eaglescliffe. Much of the town centre has been cleared and redeveloped with new housing or shopping areas and road systems, but a number of important buildings remain to give the town its distinctive atmosphere as a market and business centre which was created by the Bishops of Durham and made significant contributions to this country's scientific and industrial progress.

The Plates

Norton and Billingham

Settlements were in existence at Norton and Billingham during the Saxon period and there is evidence of Norman architecture in the churches at both places. Built on high ground at either side of Billingham Beck, they are situated a short distance to the north of Stockton with housing clustered around each village green. Stockton's growth as a business and industrial centre brought considerable housing development to the Norton area, and the establishment of I.C.I. Works at Billingham in the 1920s transformed the original settlement there.

1. The Church of St Mary the Virgin viewed from the south-east in 1900. The Saxon crossing tower is clearly visible. John Walker, inventor of the world's first friction match, is buried in the graveyard.

2. A view of St Mary's church from the south-west, showing later additions.

3. Interior of St Mary's church showing the nave crossing with pulpit, rood screen and candle chandeliers in about 1910.

4. Local inhabitants gather on Norton Green in about 1895. Notice the steam tram in the distance beyond the pond.

5. Norton Mill which stood at the bottom of Mill Lane. The first mention of a mill on this site is in the Boldon Book of 1183, and the building shown here dated from 1780. Last used in about 1910, it was damaged during a bombing raid in 1940 and demolished in 1960. The site was excavated in 1978 before the A19 Billingham Bypass was constructed across this area.

6. A painting of Norton Mill in about 1800 – one of several water mills that were built along Billingham Beck.

7. The crushing plant for Stockton Stone and Concrete Company Ltd., 1899-1967, situated on Station Road at Norton, photographed in about 1900. The site was previously occupied by the Norton Ironworks of Warner & Co., 1855-79.

8. A rare photograph of the Norton Iron Works of Warner, Lucas and Barrett on Station Road at Norton. Three blast furnaces operated on this 30-acre site between 1855 and 1879 and the original 'Big Ben' bell for Westminster, which weighed almost 16 tons, was cast here in 1856. The photograph dates from the late 1880s, just before the buildings were demolished.

9. A view of Billingham Green in the early years of this century. Properties around the green include the smithy Billingham Cash Trading Stores and the church school, as well as the cross which was erected in 1893.

10. Billingham Green in about 1910.

High Street

11. Major John Jenkins' house is pictured at the north end of the High Street. He was a Welshman in Cromwell's army and stayed in the town after the castle's demolition in 1662. His residence dated from that time, but was rebuilt in the 19th century. After his death, he left a bequest of one shilling per week to pay for white bread to feed the town's poor.

12. Drawing of the town's first almshouses, built in 1682 and replaced in 1816 with money provided by George Brown. The second building on the site was demolished in 1896 and replaced by premises in Dovecot Street.

13. View of the High Street from the southern end in 1785.

14. View of the High Street from the south in 1796.

15. North end of the High Street viewed in 1890.

16. Photograph of the north end of the High Street in 1895.

17. North end of the High Street showing Victoria Buildings, which stood on the site of the town's almshouses and were demolished in 1964.

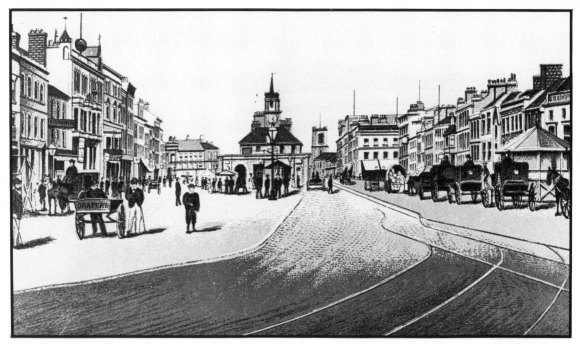

18.   Print showing the south end of the High Street in 1895. Tram lines from Yarm Lane merge with those running along the length of the High Street past the cab rank.

19.   East side of the High Street photographed in about 1890 with a steam tram. Such trams operated from October 1881 until November 1897 when they were replaced by electrically-powered trams.

20. A busy scene at the southern end of the High Street, *c.*1890. A steam tram is passing numerous horse-drawn carriages, traps and carts. The iron canopy on the left indicates the frontage of the Borough Hall, now the site of the post office. The adjacent coffee palace was one of a number of such venues in the town which opened to combat increased intemperance.

21. A similar view except that steam trams have been replaced by electrically-powered trams with overhead wires.

22. A view dated about 1900 featuring the Town Hall. The interior is larger than one might think from the outside and rooms have provided not only a meeting place for the town council but also premises for a public house, several shops, law courts and a lock-up for law breakers.

23. Photograph of the northern end of the High Street, probably taken from the top of the Town Hall early this century. Victoria Buildings on the right, with its twin domes, stands on the site of the almshouses. Robinson's Coliseum, one of the country's earliest steel-framed buildings, is on the left with a tower at the rear.

24. Looking north from the junction with Dovecot Street in about 1900. An electric tram can be seen on the right and the drum resting close to the lamp post may indicate that lighting along the High Street is in the process of being converted from gas to electricity.

25. Looking northwards along the High Street, c.1909.

26. An 1825 view of the Town Hall and doric column with Finkle Street in the centre sloping down towards the river.

27. Town Hall and doric column featured in a drawing of 1835.

28. View of the doric
column and Finkle Street on
market day.

29. A water cart sprays the
cobbled High Street near the
junction with Finkle Street
in 1914. F. Collit & Co.'s
wholesale and retail
hardware, pottery and
stationery shop occupied
part of the Town Hall
premises and Nattrass and
Granger's 'complete house
furnishing' shop is on the site
now occupied by the
Yorkshire Bank.

30. South door of the Town Hall and insignia photographed in 1910. The plaster on the insignia, which features prominently on the southern wall of the Town Hall, was reinforced with human hair.

31. View from the Town Hall looking towards the southern end of the High Street with the doric column and Shambles in the central section. This photograph dates from the 1920s.

32. Outbuildings at the rear of William IV Yard. *William IV Inn* was at No. 68 High Street from 1834-1968. Many licensed premises in the High Street area were served by outbuildings which often included stables and workshops for blacksmiths and leather-workers. This photograph was taken in the late 1960s, just before the premises were demolished for redevelopment.

33. Aerial view of the north end of the High Street dating from 1932. The parish church is prominent in the centre with the cattle market occupying the area behind the High Street shops.

34. Nos. 42 and 44 High Street were occupied by Holmes' Northern Counties Supply Stores Ltd. from 1880-1918. This photograph was taken in 1920.

35. No. 78 and adjacent business premises photographed in the early 1920s. The *Royal Hotel* operated from 1740-1962, Maison de Chapeaux 1917-22, C. W. Laws 1899-1968 and Millers' Candy Stores 1917-22. The emblem of Stockton Cycling Club is featured on the wall above C. W. Laws' premises. This section of the High Street was demolished in 1973.

36. No. 79½ photographed in 1920.

37. No. 112 where Lamplugh operated from 1902-39. This photograph dates from 1920.

38. No. 115, A. Curry & Son, butchers (1924-60), photographed in 1925.

39. Nos. 119 and 120, premises of Blackburn & Co., photographed in 1925. The business operated from 1894-1971, with a new frontage added in the 1930s. Demolition and reconstruction work followed in 1955.

40. No. 144, occupied by the Public Benefit Boot Co. Ltd. from 1896-1918, photographed *c.*1910.

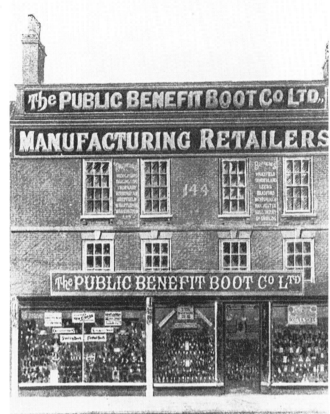

41. Nos. 91-94 High Street photographed in 1900. The Borough Hall (No.91, on the left) stood from 1850-1953, *Post Office Hotel* (No. 92) operated from 1862-97, North East Banking Company (No. 93) from 1900-21, and W. Scorer, ironmonger (No. 94) from 1894-1937. Before it became a hotel, No. 92 housed the town's post office, but in 1862 it moved to premises in the Town Hall. A new post office was built in Dovecot Street in 1880 and in 1972 the present post office building was opened on the site of No. 92 High Street.

42. Borough Hall.

43.   Regal Cinema opened on 22 April 1935 next to the Borough Hall.

44. Nos. 101-106 High Street photographed in 1939. The Dainty Confectionery Company (No. 101) was in business from 1924-81, the *Royal Exchange Hotel* (No. 102) operated from 1897-1941, Neville (boot dealer at No. 103) and Stewarts Clothiers (No. 106) from 1890-1971.

45. Nos. 135-137 High Street photographed in 1911. R. Scupham and Sons, picture-frame makers, were in business at No. 135 from 1909-18, London Joint Stock Bank Ltd. at No. 136 operated from 1909-18, and J. W. Gargett, the Hat King, was based at No. 137 from 1900-55.

46. This water pump was situated at the southern end of the High Street and was operational from 1861. The *Black Lion Hotel* is in the background, on the left.

47. The Dodshon Memorial opened for public use on 26 August 1878 and was situated in the centre of the High Street opposite the Exchange Hall. It was later moved to its present position in Ropner Park.

48. A closer view of Dodshon's Memorial dated 1880. It was erected in memory of John
Dodshon, President of the local temperance society, and included horse and dog troughs, as
well as four projecting basins with lions' heads in bronze and bronze cups for public use.

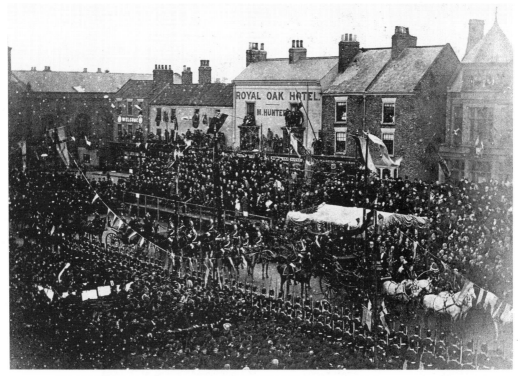

49. The visit of Their Royal Highnesses the Prince and Princess of Wales to Stockton on 21 December 1883. Princess Alexandra (1844-1925) was the daughter of King Christian IX of Denmark. She married the future king, Edward VII (1841-1910) in 1863 and they became the ruling monarchs upon the death of Queen Victoria in 1901.

50. A procession either for the Cherry Fair or Mayor's Day in about 1900 taking place in Yarm Lane close to the junction with the High Street.

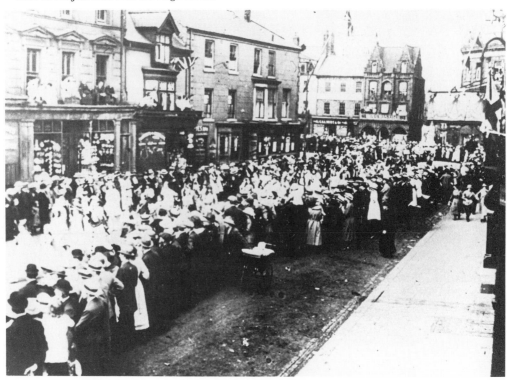

51. Crowds photographed outside the Town Hall in about 1900. They appear to be listening to speeches from the balcony on the north side of the Town Hall.

52. Stockton's Mayor, Alderman W. Newton, announcing the accession of King Edward VIII from the balcony on the north side of the Town Hall on 24 January 1936.

53.   Crowds watching a pillow fight at the Cherry Fair in about 1920.

54.   Until industrial pollution seriously affected the river in about 1920, the Tees provided fine catches of salmon and most of the fish on sale at the market was caught locally. In 1903 a pound weight of salmon is said to have cost two shillings and the photograph of the salmon stalls dates from that time. The Town Hall and Market Cross are visible in the background.

55.　The crab and winkle stall at Stockton Market in about 1920. The stall is situated just south of the Shambles, and fish was on sale from Little Brown Street to Ramsgate.

56. Crowds gather at the War Memorial just south of the parish church for the unveiling ceremony on 31 May 1923.

57. View of the platform party at the unveiling ceremony which was attended by Hensley Henson, Bishop of Durham, and the Earl of Durham.

John Walker 1781~1859

58. A metal engraving of John Walker. He did not patent his invention of the friction match and left others to gain fame and fortune from his work.

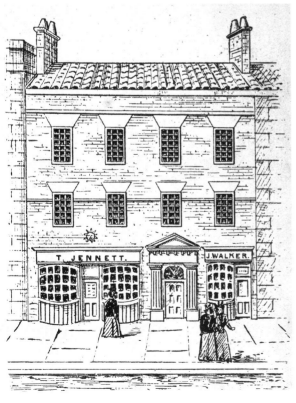

59. Nos. 56-59 High Street, Stockton. No. 59 was used by John Walker for his business as a chemist and druggist from 1819-58.

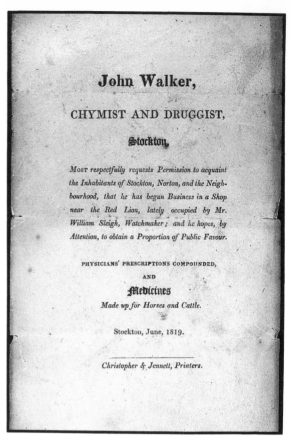

60. The interior of an apothecary's shop in the 19th century.

61. John Walker's trade card, issued after he began trading from premises at No. 59 High Street.

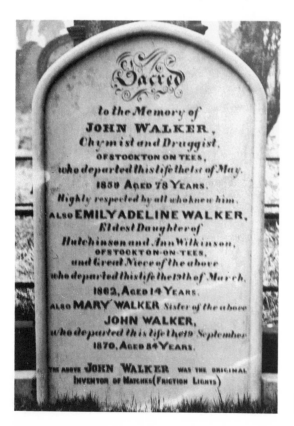

62. John Walker's gravestone in St Mary's churchyard, Norton.

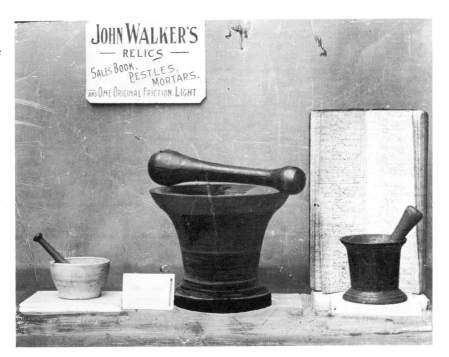

63. A chemist's pestles, mortars, day book and friction light displayed in the window of No. 58 High Street and photographed in 1927.

64. Entries in John Walker's day book for April 1827.

65. A view of The Square in 1858. It was situated east of the parish church and in later life John Walker lived in the tall house just right of centre.

Housing

66.   Mason's Court ran between the High Street and the river, opposite the Shambles. The narrow passage leading into Mason's Court was known as 'Breaky-Neck Yard'. This photograph dates from 1900.

67.   Entrance to Cherry Lane, an area now occupied by the Police Station, photographed *c*.1927.

68.   Residents of Constable's Yard photographed in 1925. A number of such yards were situated on the east side of the High Street close to the *Riverside Tavern*.

69. Wasp's Nest photographed in 1925. This thoroughfare led to the town's Georgian Theatre which operated from 1766 until the early 1870s.

70. The Square and the Thistle Green area in 1925. Stockton Police Station now covers this site.

71. No. 3 Cleveland Row photographed in 1928, shortly before demolition. Property in this area dated from the 18th century.

72. Backyard and outside lavatories photographed in 1900.

73.   Demolition of houses on Housewives Lane in the Thistle Green area. Large sectors of housing near to the river were cleared during the 1920s.

Castle Theatre

THIS STONE WAS LAID BY
MRS. RICHARD MURRAY,
OF ELM PARK, HARROGATE,
OCTOBER 3RD 1907.

74.   Dignitaries at the ceremony to mark the laying of the foundation stone of the Castle Theatre. The first play, *The Lady of Lyons*, was performed on 31 July 1908.

ERECTION OF
CASTLE THEATRE
STOCKTON 1908

75. The workforce involved with construction of the theatre. Contemporary reports indicate that they worked until 9.00 p.m. in order to complete the building work on schedule.

76. Detail of the theatre's interior. In its later years the building housed bingo sessions, but the premises were vacated in the late 1960s to make way for the *Swallow Hotel* in 1970.

77. With the advent of moving pictures, the building was renamed the Empire Theatre in about 1912 and the buildings included a large suite of billiard rooms and shops.

78. A view down Castlegate towards the river with the theatre buildings on the right-hand side.

79. These ivy-covered cottages stood on the corner of Castlegate and the High Street before the theatre was built. They were probably built in the late 17th century and faced directly up Yarm Lane.

Bridge Road

This busy thoroughfare linked the southern end of the High Street with the bridging point across the River Tees to South Stockton, renamed Thornaby in 1893.

80.   Looking north along Bridge Road towards the High Street with the Court House Buildings (built in 1863) on the left, Castle Brewery on the right and a terrace of houses completed in 1865. Distant view of the Town House and parish church. This photograph dates from 1865.

81. The High Street from Bridge Road
in about 1900. Single-storey shops occupy
what were the front gardens of two
cottages. These were cleared in 1907-8 to
make way for the Castle Theatre. The
Royal Hotel in the centre stood on this site
from 1740-1962.

82. The last surviving building of
Stockton Castle. This barn was converted
into two castellated cowhouses during
1800 on the orders of Bishop Barrington.
Situated close to the Bridge Road/Moat
Street corner, it was finally demolished
on 29 June 1865.

83. This cottage at St John's Well on Bridge Road is situated near the point where Thomas Meynell laid the first rail of the Stockton and Darlington Railway on 13 May 1822. This building is said to have been the booking office for passenger traffic on the railway, which opened on 27 September 1825.

84. Castle Brewery dominated land at the northern end of Bridge Road where Stockton Castle formerly stood. Built to a rectangular plan, this northern range of buildings included the barley store.

85. Circular tablet on the northern range with a castle motif and the lettering 'Kirk Brothers Castle Brewery'.

86. Inscribed plate giving details of the brewery's opening in 1858 under William Kilvington Kirk and John Kirk and its enlargement in 1878 by William and Thomas Lascelles Kirk. The brewery closed in 1930 and the site was cleared in 1969.

87.   Northern range of buildings from the east. Between 25 and 30 employees worked in the brewery, including eight draymen, eight workers in the maltings and eight in the brewery section.

88.   The southern range of buildings including coopers' workshop and stables to house Cleveland Bay horses. A vast network of storerooms ran under the whole site.

Bridges and the River Scene

89.   Stockton's first bridge opened on 29 April 1769, but was demolished to make way for Victoria Bridge in 1887. The abutments of this early bridge are still visible on both banks downstream from Victoria Bridge. The tall building in the distance is the Clevo Flour Mill which operated from 1871 to c.1950.

90. Victoria Bridge was opened on 20 June 1887 and replaced the earlier five-arch bridge. Until the recent county boundary changes, it linked Durham with Yorkshire.

91. An unnamed ship at Corporation Quay in the 1870s.

92.   S.S. *Stockton* pictured in the 1880s.

93.   The view downstream during the final years of the last century. The schooner in the foreground is *Young Hudson* and the vessel in the centre background is being fitted out at Craig Taylor's Shipyard. Rowing clubs and water skiers still make use of this stretch of the river and for a number of years this century the 'Tees Swim' was held between Victoria Bridge and Newport Bridge further downstream.

94.   A view looking downstream in an easterly direction, dating from the 1890s. Ships on the stocks are at Craig Taylor's Shipyard and vessels moored on the Stockton side of the river are both steam-driven and wind-powered.

95.   Quayside properties photographed during the late 19th century. The property marked with an 'x' was occupied by John Walker, inventor of the friction match.

96.   A steam-powered paddle boat at Stockton in the 1890s. It may well be the *Old Glory*, one of a number of such vessels that plied along the river between Middlesbrough and Stockton.

97.   Launch from Craig Taylor's Yard in 1910.

98. Aerial view of Stockton and the river during the 1920s. The northern end of the High Street and the parish church are at the bottom right of the photograph while chimneys of Whitwell's Thornaby Iron Works are prominent on the opposite bank.

99. Vessels moored at Corporation Quay.

100.   The *Baltic Tavern*, No. 18 Quayside, was previously named the *Blue Anchor Tavern* and dated from 1826. This photograph was taken in 1928, one year before its demolition.

101.   The *Ship Launch Inn*, No. 17 Quayside, photographed in 1928, a year before demolition. Cleveland Row is the terrace of properties to the right of the tavern.

102. Aerial view of Victoria Bridge with the *Bridge Hotel* (1870-1970) and the Clevo Flour Mills (1871-1960) visible on the Thornaby bank of the river, probably photographed in the 1930s.

103. The Waterloo Mills stood next to the *Baltic Tavern* (seen to the right of this tall building). Opened in 1780, the premises housed machinery for refining crude imported sugar. Later used by corn merchants as a granary and warehouse, the building was demolished in 1929. This photograph dates from 1910.

104. (*right*) This drawing was originally captioned 'The Old Manor House from the Quayside, Stockton', but while the Bishop of Durham's manor house or castle stood on a site at the southern end of the township, this building was not in fact part of it.

105. (*below*) Men's Home situated in The Square, founded 1906-7, closed in June 1973 and demolished during the following year. The mission next door attracted a congregation from all over the town. The building was previously a mansion and was set up to provide clean, respectable and cheap digs for shipyard workers at nearby yards.

106. (*below right*) The *Custom House Hotel* was opened in 1730 and stood at the bottom of Finkle Street (Customs officials had been moved to nearby premises in 1680). The railway track seen in the foreground ran along the quayside from St John's Crossing in Bridge Road to Corporation Quay. This building was demolished in 1970 as part of the re-development scheme.

Churches, Chapels and other Places of Worship

107. The parish church at the northern end of the High Street which replaced a chapel of ease. Building work began in 1710 and the church was consecrated on 21 August 1712. This photograph dates from about 1900.

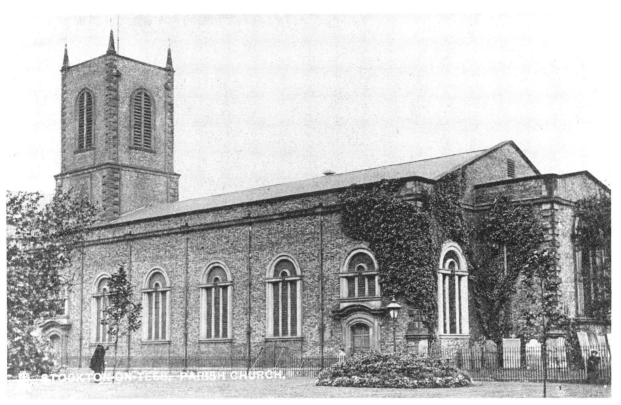

108.   View from the churchyard close to the probable site of the chapel of ease.

109.   This photograph shows the new chancel which dates from 1906.

110. View of the parish church showing the rebuilt chancel of 1906 and the side chapel dating from 1925. The war memorial was erected in 1923.

111. Interior of the parish church showing the altar and chancel.

112. Holy Trinity church, opened in 1838 on land granted by the Bishop of Durham in 1832.

113. Holy Trinity church pulpit and pews.

114. Decorative doorways of the Baptist Tabernacle. Design work was carried out by T. W. T. Richardson.

115. Baptist Tabernacle on Wellington Street, opened 1902.

116. Holy Trinity vicarage, Yarm Lane, demolished in 1980.

117. St John's church, near the town's railway station, was opened in 1874, closed in 1978 and demolished in 1980. An interesting feature was the building's basilican style.

118. St Peter's church. The foundation stone was laid in 1880 and the new church was consecrated on 13 October 1881 by Bishop Lightfoot.

119. Interior of St Peter's church. The architect was Mr. E. E. Clephan and the style is Early English.

120.   Modern business premises in the former Paradise Row Primitive Methodist church on Church Road, which opened in 1866 and closed in 1945.

121.   The Society of Friends Meeting House on Dovecot Street. The original building dated from 1814 and a two-storey brown brick façade was added in 1840.

Stockton and Thornaby Hospital

Stockton Surgical Hospital was originally built in 1862 on a site close to the river. Building work got underway on a new site adjacent to Bowesfield Lane during 1875 and the first patients were admitted some two years later.

122. Nursing staff and patients in the grounds of the hospital's Bowesfield Lane site.

123. View of the main blocks flanking the entrance building. The hospital closed in 1974 and the site was cleared during 1977. Housing development now covers this area.

124. Scenes from hospital life on the Bowesfield Lane site.

125. The Children's Ward during 1919 or 1920. Nurses McKenzie and Wetherall are pictured with patients. The boy with the guitar, Jack Maxwell, was recovering from a broken leg and Dorothy Smith (right of centre, with head bandages) was convalescing after a mastoid operation. She recalls that her grandmother cycled from the family home at Brompton every Saturday, Sunday and Wednesday for visiting. Hospital meals were really appreciated – notably the rice pudding and mince meat – and the girls had a clean red ribbon put in their hair daily to match the red bedjackets that they wore.

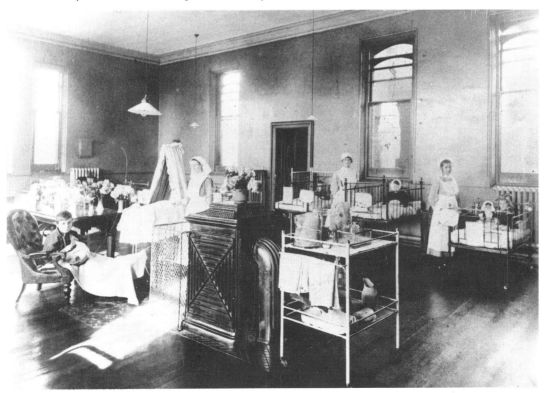

Sports Teams and Theatrical Groups

126.   Players and spectators at the Stockton Corporation Cricket Match in 1894. The match may have taken place at the old cricket ground close to Norton Road just beyond Lustrum Beck.

127.   The Corporation Officials' Football Team which beat a police eleven by two goals to one on 14 March 1895 on the Victoria Ground. Back row, from left to right: Mr. J. Reay, W. Reay, H. K. Kindler, W. Brown, Councillor Barn. Middle row: J. Urwin, H. E. Aston, R. Ainsworth. Front row: W. H. Nattrass, A. Richardson, C. W. Cockersoll, W. Barn, T. H. Salmon (?). This sporting venue was closed and redeveloped with housing in the 1970s.

128.   Stockton Cherry Fair dates back to the 18th century, if not earlier, and races were held annually on 18 July under the supervision of a clerk of the sports. The venue is the Victoria Football Ground in 1904 and donkey races are about to get underway.

129.   Members of Norton Hill football club photographed during the 1906-7 season. The team played on a pitch which was situated on land opposite the *Brown Jug* public house on Norton Road.

130.   Holy Trinity Church Choir Cricket XI photographed at Elton Hall in 1920 during a match versus Maurice Ropner's X

131. Local youngsters appearing in a play 'Jan of Windmill Lane' at Holy Trinity Hall in 1928. The producer was Will Hewitt.

132.   The cast of 'Princess Ju-Ju' – an operetta performed on 25/26 April 1928 at Holy Trinity Hall and again produced by Will Hewitt.

133.   Members of Stockton Rotary Club in 1928.

Hartburn

Hartburn, formerly known as East Hartburn, was a small agricultural community about two miles west of Stockton's High Street which became a popular residential district for business people and industrialists. Several large properties were built during the late 19th and early 20th centuries, including Hartburn Lodge on Harsley Road. The main building, stable block and extensive grounds of the Lodge were completed after 1903 for the Raimes family who had business interests in central Stockton. Photographs of the grounds and building are in the possession of Mrs. R. Hill whose grandfather, John Albert Warren, worked as estate agent, head gardener and bailiff on the Raimes' estates at Hartburn and Acaster Malbis near York.

134. Entrance porch and view of Hartburn Lodge from the west. The initials and figures 'FR 1903 MR' are carved in stone above the main entrance and in the wood panelling of the entrance hall.

135.   Stable block adjacent to Hartburn Lodge.

136.   View from the south. The external features are unaltered, except for the removal of the conservatory (extreme right) and balcony (extreme left). The building is now a children's home owned by Cleveland County Council.

137.   The Oak Room, including an impressive fireplace and woodwork.

138.   The Drawing Room.

139. Entrance Hall.

140. View from the south-west.

141. Family group at the lake in the grounds of Hartburn Lodge. From left to right are: Mr. and Mrs. Nattrass (daughter and son-in-law of Mrs. Raimes), Mrs. Raimes, Mrs. John Albert Warren and Elsie Cornwall Warren.

142. The Lodge and the driveway leading on to Harlsey Road.

143. View of Hartburn Lodge from Harlsey Road
– with unmade road surface.

144. Harper Terrace in Hartburn Village in 1905,
showing Mrs. John Albert Warren, Harry
Cornwall Warren and Elsie Cornwall Warren
outside the family home.

145.   Class from Hartburn school in about 1898. Rhoda Featherstone is second from the left in the front row of seated pupils.

146. Class from Hartburn school in 1900. The Headmistress at the time was Mrs. Parncutt. This red-brick building was opened on 12 January 1877 and for a number of years it also served as a mission hall, but when the day school moved out in 1911 the building was converted for use as a place of worship. Bishop H. C. G. Moule of Durham performed the dedication ceremony on 24 June 1913.

147. Hartburn Bridge carried the Stockton to Castle Eden Railway across Hartburn Bank. Constructed in 1877, it was a fine example of a Victorian skew-arch bridge, but caused continual traffic problems and following closure of the railway in 1968, the bridge was demolished during February 1975. Note also the horse trough in the middle distance. It was provided by Charles Arthur Head of Hartburn Hall to refresh horses negotiating the steep, twisting bank.

148. The lake in Ropner Park. Land was donated by the Ropner family and the park was opened for public use on 4 October 1883 by the Duke and Duchess of York, later King George V and Queen Mary. Large residences in Oxbridge Lane are to be seen to the right of centre.

149. A view from Ropner Park in 1911. The ornamental fountain has recently been restored, but the cannon disappeared many years ago.

150. The bandstand and nearby open-air theatre, built in 1951, have both been demolished.

Scenes around Stockton

151. A steam tram photographed at the Stockton Depot in 1885. These trams had a short operational span from October 1881 to November 1897 when the power source was changed to electricity.

152. Laying new tram lines at the northern end of Norton High Street during the early weeks of 1898. Steam trams which worked on a 4ft.-gauge ended operations on Christmas Eve 1897 and the electric trams which replaced them used a 3 ft. 7in.-gauge. The new service using electric trams began on 16 July 1898.

153. Electric trams Nos. 22 and 24 photographed on Norton High Street in about 1900.

154. Norton tram sub-station photographed in about 1900.

155. Norton tram terminus at the northern end of the High Street. Robinsons' café is clearly visible in the centre of the photograph with the *Hambletonian Inn* and the Clock Building in the distance. The photograph dates from 1910.

156. Norton Road in about 1895 featuring the elegant properties of North Terrace and Victoria Terrace. North Terrace Wesleyan Chapel (left) was built in 1866 and demolished in 1955; St Mary's Roman Catholic Church was built in 1844. Tracks for steam trams can be seen in the centre of the road.

157. A photograph taken in July 1898 looking towards the High Street from Norton Road. J. T. Inglis' premises were a tobacconist's shop and the building behind the tram was Arundale's *Talbot Inn*.

158. Sheep being herded towards the cattle market on Church Road, *c.*1903.

159. Geese on their way to market early this century. In the weeks before Christmas flocks of over one hundred geese were driven into the market for sale. They were not kept in pens, but held in a flock by the use of a long switch cut from a tree. The birds were 'shod' before arrival by dipping their feet in warm tar and then sand.

160. During 1935, Church Road was widened by moving the church wall. The old cattle market is visible in the middle distance beyond the parish church.

161. Sheep being herded along Church Row (now Church Road) towards the High Street in about 1904. The *Castle and Anchor Inn* is on the left and chimneys of the Stockton Malleable Iron Works dominate the middle distance.

162. The imposing doorway and windows of the town's former police station in Church Road. In its early days it was used as a collegiate school run by Mr. Charles Cooke and, after service as a police station from 1877-1973, it now forms the east wing of the housing department.

163. A closer view of the police station in Church Road. This photograph which dates from 1944 shows the measures that were taken to protect the doorway and windows from bomb damage during air raids.

164. The Plaza Theatre in Bishop Street operated from 1936 untl 1959, after which it was used for storage until this area was cleared for redevelopment in 1970. The Royal Star Theatre was opened on this site in 1878 but, after a serious fire in 1883, it re-opened as 'The Grand Theatre of Varieties'. The premises were adapted as a cinema with the addition of a projection room (in the centre of the building's exterior).

165. Workers at J. F. Smith & Co.'s Nebo Confectionery Works which operated from 1920 until 1972 in premises at the top end of Theatre Yard. The building was first used as a tithe barn from about 1574, opened as a theatre in 1766 and was used by the Salvation Army before J. F. Smith & Co. moved in. This photograph gives a good indication of the processes involved in producing the confectionery. Mints or sweets have been boiled and are now being hammered or chopped ready to pack into jars which stand ready on the shelves.

166.   No. 9 Finkle Street, said to be Stockton's oldest house and probably built with stone from the castle. It dates from the late 17th century and was the residence of Edmund Harvey (1698-1781) who provided schooling on Sundays for 12 poor children. Through the years it has housed a variety of businesses and since recent restoration work, which has preserved many original features, it has been used as a coffee house.

167.   Early view of Brown's Bridge on Bishopton Road, one of the main routes out of Stockton. It crossed the Lustrum Beck and was built in 1790. A modern bridge of 1903 has replaced this structure. Wren's Mill may be clearly seen in the background.

168. A view of Yarm Road looking towards central Stockton with the spire of Yarm Road Methodist church and the tower of St Peter's church in the distance. Richard Hind School opened on 14 January 1913 and was an elementary school until January 1922 when it became a selective central school. It closed in December 1979 and the site was cleared for housing development.

169. The Queen Victoria High School for Girls, situated on Yarm Road, was opened on 28 October 1905 by Princess Henry of Battenburg. It joined with the Cleveland School to form the Teesside High School at Eaglescliffe in 1970 and the premises were demolished to make way for a modern public house which continues the royal title.

170. The Old National School (St Thomas')
erected in 1846 in The Square at the end of
Smithfield.

171. Stockton Higher
Grade School. Building
work spanned the years
1892-6 and the architect was
Mr. J. M. Bottomley. The
premises became Stockton
Secondary Grammar School
and achieved a fine
academic standing. In 1951
grammar school pupils
moved to new premises at
Grangefield and Stockton-
Billingham Technical
College used the premises
between 1951-75. During the
late 1970s Stockton's
Further Education
Department was based here,
but following closure in 1980
the building was demolished
during the winter months of
1984-5.

172.   This stone tablet was built into the red-brick frontage of the former Higher Grade School on Nelson Terrace. The building became structurally unsafe and was demolished in 1984-5.

173.   Bowesfield Lane photographed during the 1850s or 1860s. In earlier days this thoroughfare was known as 'Love' or 'Lovesome' Lane.

174. John Bowron's stone and marble yard on Yarm Lane. A stone mason is at work in this photograph which dates from about 1890.

175. Frontage of the former town library on the north side of Wellington Street. Built in 1870 as a hall for the Freemasons, it was demolished after the library was moved to new premises on Church Road.

176. Properties on Brunswick Street, erected in about 1820 and demolished in 1963.

177. Elegant doorways are a feature of Nos. 9 and 10 on Brunswick Street.

178. The town's fire station was opened in West Row in 1883. In previous years the fire engine had been based in a corner of the parish churchyard. The stone tablet contains the insignia of a castle and anchor which appears on several buildings in the town. It denotes Stockton's development as a port after its early establishment under the Bishops of Durham with their manor house or castle.

179. Stockton's engine sheds and locomotives in about 1939.

180. One of Stockton's landmarks, the *Queen's Hotel*, which stood close to the railway station. This photograph dates from the early 1900s and the site has now been cleared following a serious fire in 1981.

181. The Masonic Hall on the north side of Wellington Street. Freemasonry was established in Stockton at the *Queen's Head Tavern*, Portrack, in 1756 and they used several premises in the town, including the *Black Lion* and the *Vane Arms*, before moving into a hall on the north side of Wellington Street. The first meeting in the present building took place in 1876.

Bibliography

Books

Brewster, John, *The parochial history and antiquities of Stockton-upon-Tees*.
Fordyce, William, *History and Antiquities of the County Palatine of Durham* (1857).
Graves, Rev., *The History of Cleveland* (Reprint 1972).
Heavisides, Michael, *The Condensed History of Stockton-on-Tees* (1917).
Morris, John (ed.), *Boldon Book* (1982).
North, G. A., *Teesside's Economic Heritage* (1975).
Pevsner, Nikolaus, *The Buildings of England – County Durham* (1983).
Richmond, Thomas, *Local Records of Stockton and the Neighbourhood* (1868).
Sowler, Tom, *A History of the Town and Borough of Stockton-on-Tees* (1972).
Stockton-on-Tees Railway Centenary Committee, *The Railway Centenary 1825-1925* (1925).
Woodhouse, Robert, *Cleveland's Hall of Fame (and Infamy)* (1987).

Local guides and monographs

Sowler, Tom, *The Parish Church of Stockton-on-Tees*.
Sowler, Tom, *Town House, Stockton-on-Tees*.
Towlard, Dennis, *The Stockton Georgian Theatre*.
Woodhouse, Robert, *Discovering Cleveland* (1978).
Woodhouse, Robert, *History of Stockton Castle* (1967).
Stockton-on-Tees Official Guide.

Articles

Various published in issues of Cleveland and Teesside Local History Society – see index for issues 1-50 June 1968-Spring 1986.

Miscellaneous

Evening Gazette, Middlesbrough.
Woodhouse, Robert, *Stockton-on-Tees – A Personal View*.
The Stockton Scene published by Scenic Stockton, 1978.
The Stockton Borough Trail published by Scenic Stockton, 1978.
The Stockton Township Trail published by Scenic Stockton, 1978.